The story of Daniel in the lions' den is retold
in this delightfully simple version and will appeal
to all young listeners and early readers.
The story is based on the Book of Daniel, Chapter 6.

LADYBIRD BOOKS, INC.
Lewiston, Maine 04240 U.S.A.
© LADYBIRD BOOKS LTD MCMLXXXV
Loughborough, Leicestershire, England
© Illustrations LYNN N. GRUNDY MCMLXXXV

Printed in England

Daniel

written by HY MURDOCK
illustrated by LYNN N. GRUNDY

Ladybird Books

When Daniel was a boy, he lived in Jerusalem, but one day an army from Babylonia captured the city.

The King of Babylon took many people back to his own country to work for him. Young Daniel and his family had to go, too. Daniel had to work in the king's palace.

The people in this new land didn't pray to God. Daniel had been taught about God, and even though he was in a strange land, he still remembered to say his prayers every day.

Years went by, and Daniel became a man. He and his friends were very clever and worked hard at the king's palace. Daniel was good at everything he did and never made mistakes.

Soon he became very important and helped King Darius rule the country. Still Daniel remembered to pray to God every day.

When the king's other helpers saw how much the king liked Daniel, they were jealous. They said that Daniel did not belong to their country, yet now he was more important than they were.

They tried to catch Daniel doing something wrong so that they could tell the king and get Daniel into trouble. But Daniel didn't make any mistakes.

One day they saw Daniel praying to God, and this gave them an idea. They went to see the king. ''We think you should make a new law so that all the people will obey you. For the next thirty days no one must ask for help from anyone but you. If anyone breaks this law, he will be thrown into the lions' den.''

King Darius didn't know that this was a plot against Daniel, so he signed the law.

Daniel heard about the new law, but he still asked God to help him in his work. Daniel's enemies saw him praying and went to tell the king.

"Daniel is breaking the law. He is asking his God for help," they said. "You must throw him into the den of lions." King Darius knew that he had been tricked. He was very sad because he loved Daniel, and now Daniel had to be thrown to the lions.

The lions were fierce and hungry, and Daniel was frightened. He knew that only God could save him, so he began to pray.

King Darius couldn't eat or sleep that night because he was so worried.

Early in the morning he went to see what had happened to Daniel. He shouted to see whether Daniel was still alive, and Daniel answered, ''My God has saved me.''

The king was very happy and told the men to pull Daniel out of the den. He said that Daniel's enemies should be put in the lions' den instead.

Now that King Darius had seen how God had taken care of Daniel, he said that all his people must pray to Daniel's God.